PowerKiDS
Readers

SEA FRIENDS
LOS AMIGOS DEL MAR

MANATEES
LOS MANATÍES

SAM DRUMLIN
TRADUCCIÓN AL ESPAÑOL: EDUARDO ALAMÁN

PowerKiDS
press™

New York

Published in 2013 by The Rosen Publishing Group, Inc.
29 East 21st Street, New York, NY 10010

First Edition

Editor: Amelie von Zumbusch
Book Design: Liz Gloor and Colleen Bialecki   Traducción al español: Eduardo Alamán

Photo Credits: Cover Perrine Doug/Perspectives/Getty Images; p. 5 Comstock/Thinkstock; p. 7 Steffen Foerster Photography/Shutterstock.com; p. 9 iStockphoto/Thinkstock; p. 11 Photo Researchers/Getty Images; pp. 13, 23 A Cotton Photo/Shutterstock.com; p. 15 Shane Gross/Shutterstock.com; p. 17 Undersea Discoveries/Shutterstock.com; p. 19 Douglas Faulkner/Photo Researchers/Getty Images; p. 21 Romarti/Shutterstock.com.

Library of Congress Cataloging-in-Publication Data

Drumlin, Sam.
  [Manatees. English & Spanish]
  Manatees = Los manatíes / by Sam Drumlin ; translated by Eduardo Alamán. — 1st ed.
     p. cm. — (Powerkids readers: sea friends = Los amigos del mar)
  Includes index.
  ISBN 978-1-4488-9974-6 (library binding)
  1. Manatees—Juvenile literature. I. Title. II. Title: Manatíes.
  QL737.S63D7818 2013
  599.55–dc23

                                    2012022772

Web Sites: Due to the changing nature of Internet links, PowerKids Press has developed an online list of Web sites related to the subject of this book. This site is updated regularly. Please use this link to access the list: www.powerkidslinks.com/pkrsf/mana/

Manufactured in the United States of America

CPSIA Compliance Information: Batch #W13PK3: For Further Information contact Rosen Publishing, New York, New York at 1-800-237-9932

CONTENTS

Manatees 4
Beware of Boats 16
Calves 18
Words to Know 24
Index 24

CONTENIDO

Manatíes 4
Cuidado con los barcos 16
Crías 18
Palabras que debes saber 24
Índice 24

Manatees live in warm water.

Los **manatíes** viven en el agua templada.

They can live in rivers or in the sea.

Pueden vivir en ríos o en el mar.

They are also called sea cows.

También se los conoce como vacas marinas.

There are three kinds
of manatees.

Existen tres clases
de manatíes.

They eat **plants**.

Los manatíes comen **plantas**.

They are big and gentle.

Son grandes y bonachones.

Boats often hurt them.

Con frecuencia, los barcos los lastiman.

Babies are **calves**.

Los bebés son las **crías**.

They drink milk.

Los bebés beben leche.

They can live for up to 60 years.

Los manatíes pueden vivir hasta 60 años.

23

WORDS TO KNOW /
PALABRAS QUE DEBES SABER

calf / (la) cría

manatee / manatí

plants / (las) plantas

INDEX

C
calves, 18

K
kinds, 10

M
milk, 20

P
plants, 12

ÍNDICE

B
bebés, 18

L
leche, 20

P
plantas, 12

T
tipos, 10